The Capital Flight Plan: Navigating Your Path to Financial Freedom

Introduction — Your Escape Plan to Financial Freedom

It was a hot summer day in 2015, and Alex was stuck in traffic on his way to work. His car's air was loud, his gas was low, and his email was full of "need now" messages before he got to work. As he saw the long row of red lights ahead, he thought hard: Is this all there is?

Alex wasn't poor. He had a good job, a paycheck that paid the bills, and some money saved up. But he felt stuck—tied to a timetable not his own, a boss who set his value, and a life that needed more cash each year to stay the same. Like many others, Alex worked a lot but received little in return.

At that time, Alex didn't see he was in a cycle: make, spend, owe, do it again. It was only when he found out about financial freedom that things turned around. In seven years, by changing how he earned, saving a lot, and using his money well, Alex left his daily job and made his own life.

This book aims to help you do that, too.

Why Most People Never Escape

THE HARD FACT IS THAT many do not get to be free with money because they are using rules made by others. As kids, we learn: go to school, find a steady job, buy a home, save for our old days, and then, at 65, we can start to enjoy life.

But here's the issue: that plan was not made for you. It was made for a time that is now past. Back then, there were pensions, paying for health care was easy, and costs did not go up faster than pay. Today, taking the "usual way" can lead not to a safe place but to feeling worn out, being in debt, and putting off your dreams.

To get free, you need a new plan. Think of it as a new way to fly.

The Capital Flight Plan Mindset

THINK ABOUT BEING FREE with money, like making a plane get ready to fly. You need:

1. Fuel (Money & Savings): The power that drives your trip.

1. Map (Set Goals & Plan): A way to keep you on track.

1. Height (Money in stocks & Things you own): This lets you go high and helps your cash work hard.

1. Safety (Watch out for risk): Plans to keep your cash safe when bad times hit.

If you miss any of these four, you stay still. With them all, you pick up speed, take off, and at last, freely pick where you land.

Your Early Freedom Number

ONE OF THE FIRST STEPS is to find your free number—the cash you need to live without a job.

Here's an easy way to figure it out:

1. Note your monthly costs (home, food, bills, insurance, fun).

1. Take off what you don't need.

1. Times that number by 12.

That's your yearly base free number.

Example: If you do well on $3,000 a month, your yearly number is $36,000. Now think: What mix of money-making ways or life changes could make up that $36,000?

Most people don't ask this—and so they never make a true exit plan.

Shifting From Worker to Builder

A BIG CHANGE IN HOW you think is knowing that just a job won't set you free. Jobs are made to give you just enough cash to keep you there, but not enough to break free.

Instead, real freedom is in making:

- Things like houses, stocks that pay part of their profits, or digital things that bring in cash.
- Ways of doing things that work on their own, like saving money without thinking about it, or web shops.
- Skills that you can use in many places or across countries.

The point is to go from just working to being someone who builds stuff that keeps making value long after you start.

Quick Wins You Can Apply Today

TO START MAKING IT real from the start, here are three simple steps for this week:

1 Look at what you spent. Check out how you spent your money in the last 30 days. Find any cash that didn't help your happiness, health, or plans. Stop one of these money-wasting wastes right away.

2 Save the first 10% right away. If you make $1,000, set up a plan to put $100 into a savings or investing pot right when you get your pay. You won't miss it, and it will grow faster than you think.

3 Try a tiny side job. Use two hours this week to try out a small money idea—like online work, selling something you don't use, or making a digital item. Even making $20 on the side can change your thinking to: I can make money by myself.

These aren't huge changes yet, but they show the way.

Why This Book Will Be Different

YOU'VE LIKELY SEEN many money guides with lots of big ideas, unclear pushes, or hard charts that are just too much. This isn't like those.

This is a set of tools, not a study book. Each part aims to give you a real edge—a plan, routine, or way you can use right now. See it as your guide to money freedom.

By the end of this book, you won't just get the idea of financial freedom—you'll have a clear money flight plan made for your life. A path you can walk, where every move pushes you forward until you take off.

The Takeoff Starts Now

THINK OF A DAY WHEN you wake up and know you don't have to be stuck in cars unless you want to. Think of a day when you can move to a new land, do your work, or be more with the ones you love the most—no need to ask anyone.

That is what being free with your money means: you can choose.

This book is your way out. You don't have to wait until you are old at 65. You don't need a lot of cash saved up. What you do need is to see things, have a plan, and be ready to make moves.

Now, with this Plan to move your capital into your hands, you are on your way.

Chapter 1 — Rewriting the Rules: Defining Your Freedom Number

On a cold night in Chicago, Maya sat near her friend in a busy diner, looking at her bill. She just paid $24 for a salad and iced tea—a cost that, two years ago, would have bought three full days of food when she was abroad. She wasn't out of cash—she had a good job, a nice place, and a gym pass she hardly used. Yet, she felt unsure.

"Why does it seem like I'm on a treadmill that keeps going faster?" she asked.

Her friend just said, "That's how the city is. You work, you pay, you move on."

But deep down, Maya was not okay with "how the city is." She wanted to know: How much cash would it take to get out of this loop? Not just when old, but earlier.

That question—What's my freedom number?—was the key change.

Why "More" Is Never the Answer

MOST PEOPLE ANSWER financial uncertainty with one default response: *I just need more money.* More income, more savings, more side hustles. But "more" is a moving target.

If you don't define what "enough" looks like, lifestyle creep takes over. A raise turns into a bigger apartment, a bonus becomes a fancier car, and soon you're running faster just to stay in the same place. The system is designed to encourage endless consumption.

Your **freedom number** is the antidote. It's the exact dollar amount you need to cover your essential life costs and live comfortably—without relying on a paycheck. Once you know it, every decision becomes sharper. You stop chasing "more" and start chasing "enough."

How to Calculate Your Freedom Number

LET'S MAKE THIS CLEAR. Your free number is tied to two things:

1. What does it cost for you to live?
2. How much money do you need to keep going?

Step 1: Check Your Freedom

Pull up your bank records from the past 90 days. Mark each cost. Then, for each, ask three things:

- Did this buy make me happy for a long time?
- Could I find it cheaper but just as good?
- Would this buy still be key if I had no job?

You might find, 20–30% of your money can be cut without hurting how well you live.

For example, Maya saw she was using $400 a month on takeout because she felt "too tired to cook." By making meals twice a week, she cut that in half—saving $2,400 a year without losing out.

Step 2: Find Your Basic Free Number

Add your needs: the home, water and power, food, cover plans, getting around, doctor visits, and small fun buys. Then, times the total by 12.

Like this:

- Home: $1,200
- Water and power: $200
- Food: $500
- Cover plans: $250
- Getting around: $300
- Doctor visits: $200
- Small fun buys: $300

Total = $2,950/month → $35,400/year

That's your key number. Note, it's way less than what folks think they "need."

Step 3: Work Out Your Safety Extra

Life can surprise you. Add a 20–25% extra for sudden needs, price jumps, and more room to move. In this way, Maya's new free number came to about $44,000/year.

Why This Number Changes Everything

HERE'S THE TRICK: FIND out your freedom number, and watch how money choices change.

- That new job? Check it against what you need, not just the pay on the table.
- That side gig? Figure out how much time it cuts from your wait.

- That cost? Ask yourself, "Does this get me free quicker, or slow me down?"

Now, money makes sense. It's like a score, showing how close you are to being free.

The Power of the "Half-Freedom Number"

HERE'S A SMART PLAN: don't just figure out your total freedom number—also think about your half-freedom number.

Why? Because some freedom is often near and can come way quicker than full, total independence.

For Maya, her halfway point was around $22,000 a year. This meant that if she could grow her savings or find extra money in ways to cover just half of what she needs, she could cut down her work time, switch to an easier job, or even talk about working from far away. Even a bit of freedom makes a big change in your life.

Action Plan: Defining Your Number This Week

1. Fill out the Freedom Audit. Note all the money you use for a month. Mark any cost that didn't make your life better.

1. Set Your Base. Mix must-have items and happy buys. Be super clear—don't throw in stuff just to show off.

1. Put in Your Safety Net. Times it by 1.25 to have extra space.

1. Note It. Write your freedom number on a sticky note, phone screen, or in a diary. It's more than just numbers—it guides you.

A Real-Life Example

THINK OF TOM, A 40-year-old boss of IT. He thought he had to make at least $100,000 a year to live free. But after checking his spending, he saw he used too much on stuff he didn't need—Uber trips, boxes by mail, and paying a lot for debt. How much did he need? $38,000. With some wiggle room: $48,000.

This new info changed his life. Instead of waiting many years, Tom made a list of houses for rent that brought in $50,000 each year after only eight years. He quit working at 48—nearly 20 years sooner than he first thought he could.

Rewriting the Rules

THE OLD WAY TELLS YOU: work long, save hard, and wish for the best. But knowing your freedom number changes the game. It makes a dream that is hard to see into a clear goal.

When you know your number, you're not just watching another's game. You're making your way out, piece by piece.

So stop for a bit. Get some paper. Check your numbers. The faster you find your freedom number, the faster you can begin to close the space between where you stand now and the life you aim for.

Chapter 2 — The Income Blueprint: Building Multiple Streams

It was a wet Monday when Ethan was at his desk, reading a work email: "We are sad to say that due to changes, we have cut your job."

In just a few short minutes, the job he had had for 12 years was no more. He had some money saved, enough for a few months. But fear took over. House rent, bills, his girl's school fees—all now hung on a thin line of cash that had just run out.

Later, Ethan would say this was the day he opened his eyes. He got that true safety with money does not come from just one pay. It comes from having many ways to make money. That's when he quit asking, "How can I make more at work?" and started asking, "How can I build a way to have money come from many sides—even if one stops?"

This part of the book is your guide to doing the same thing.

The Fragility of a Single Stream

PICTURE YOUR MONEY flow as rivers going into a lake. If you just count on one river and it stops, the lake goes away too. But with five or six rivers, some large, some tiny, the lake will stay full, even if one stops.

A lot of folks see their job pay as their sole revenue. Yet, real money freedom shows up when you make sure you have more ways to get cash. This helps you stay steady if a job loss, a bad market, or a sudden big problem hits.

The Four Categories of Income Streams

LET'S MAKE IT SIMPLE. All the ways to make money come under four key types:

1. Earned Income - Cash you get for your time (jobs, side gigs, advice giving).

1. Investment Income - Cash that comes from owning things (shares, loans, extras from shares).

1. Business/Side Hustle - Money from big or small firms you run (online shops, web lessons, client services).

1. Passive/Residual Income - Cash that keeps coming even when you stop the early work (book fees, house rents, set-and-forget firms).

The plan is not to get great at all four right away. Instead, mix them one by one—so your money base grows but doesn't crush you.

Start With the "Sidecar Stream"

A SMART MOVE: SET UP a Sidecar Stream—a small, safe money source that follows your main work. This could be:

- Doing freelance work in your field on weekends.
- Leading an online course in something you know well.
- Selling digital designs, downloads, or how-tos on Etsy.
- Letting out an extra room or your car.

The goal is to start something quickly with little cost. Even $500 a month makes a difference—it's a plane ticket, a part of your rent, or money added to your investments.

Take Ethan, for example. He began teaching coding online two evenings a week. In half a year, it paid for his car and boosted his confidence to grow more.

The "Skill Flip" Strategy

A LOT OF US DON'T SEE how good we are with the skills we have. The Skill Flip means making what you know into a product or service.

Examples:

- A graphic artist makes logo templates on Canva to sell on the web.
- A teacher turns her lesson plans into a digital course.
- A fitness fan pens a $9 e-book on fast workouts for busy moms and dads.

Don't chase new fields. Instead, turn your knowledge into something you can sell again and again.

Automating Streams for Sustainability

THE STRONGEST WATER flows on, even when you aren't at work. Use automation to help you here.

- Investing: Set up auto pay into index funds or stocks that give dividends.

- Digital Products: Make it once, sell endlessly with help from auto delivery.

- Rental Real Estate: Hire property managers or use tools from Airbnb for automation.

This isn't about "do nothing and grow rich"—it's about doing tough setup tasks one time, then letting systems do the work over and over.

Case Study: The 3-Layer System

THINK ABOUT LAURA, a nurse who felt unsafe. To be safe, she set up her money in three parts:

1. Part 1: Job Money – Her nurse's job paid for her needs.

1. Part 2: Extra Money – She started a class on weekends to help new nurses with their test prep, making $600 each month.

1. Part 3: Easy Money – She got a small two-part house, lived in one side, rented the other, and set payments to go out on their own.

In four years, Laura did not just live off her nurse pay. Even without her job, her extra money was 70% of what she needed to live free.

Action Steps: Building Your Blueprint

1. Check What You Can Do & Have

- Make a list of all things you're good at and things you own (skills, land, gear, fun stuff).

- Think: "Can this help others make money?"

1. Pick a Side Job

• Choose the easiest idea.

• Start quick—even if it's not perfect. Making $100 is a big deal.

1. Make Things Easy

• Use apps, planners, or online tools to cut down on hard work.

• For example, use Gumroad to send out digital items by itself.

1. Add More Over Time

• Try to get a new way to make money each year.

• By year five, you'll have lots going on.

Breaking the Myth: You Don't Need Millions

HERE'S THE THING: YOU don't have to be super rich to stop working soon. You just need steady flows of money to meet your free-to-live goal.

Ethan made three flows—coding classes, a tiny SaaS app, and cash from shares. Together, they made $50,000 a year. That was his goal. He didn't get lucky with big money or make a huge company. He just added flows until it worked for him.

The Takeaway

LIVING ON JUST ONE paycheck is like having a house with only one support. It may hold up for some time, but if that support breaks, the whole thing falls. Having many ways to make money sets you up to be free from money worries.

Your plan isn't for fast cash—it's to build a strong, bendy way to earn that gets better as you do. Start little. Put another way, to make money. Then one more. Soon, you'll see that being free isn't about chance—it's about having a good setup.

Chapter 3 — The Saving Engine: Supercharging Your Cash Flow

On a bright Saturday morning, Mia sat at her kitchen table, drinking coffee and looking at her bank app. She made $80,000 a year—but still, by month's end, she had almost no money left.

She was not careless. She did not buy fancy cars or high-end bags. But she saw her money slip away in many small ways: old subscriptions she forgot, too many takeout meals, quick buys online. It was not that she did not make enough—it was that she did not use her money right.

When Mia took charge of her money, she did not feel cut off. She felt strong. In 18 months, she saved $25,000 without making more money. That cash helped her buy her first rental home.

Here is a hidden truth about being rich: it's not about making more—it's about keeping what you make. Saving is not just about cutting costs; it's about making your money work so each dollar helps you break free.

Cash Flow Is Your Freedom Engine

THINK OF YOUR CASH as gas. If you use it all in small goes—like on quick food, or stuff you don't use—you won't have much for a big trip. But if you put that gas into a strong motor, you make it move.

The saving motor isn't about being tight. It's about moving lost cash toward your free goal. The quicker you save, the sooner you break free.

The Rule of 20% Redirect

HERE'S A SMART TIP: plan to put 20% of your money towards freedom.

If you make $3,000 a month → $600 should go into investments, paying off debt, or side jobs.

If that seems too hard, begin with 5%, then grow. The aim is to get better, not to be perfect.

Why 20%? Because a lot of us use up our whole paycheck. At 20%, you give yourself some space without giving up too much. Over time, this 20% grows a lot due to compounding.

Stop the Leaks: The Silent Cash Killers

BEFORE BOOSTING YOUR savings, first stop the waste. These are tiny, but steady costs that quietly take your money away.

1. Old subscriptions – Check every 90 days. If you aren't using it, stop it.

1. Spending more as you earn more – When you get a raise, try not to increase your spending too.

1. Big interest debts – Credit cards at 20% APR eat your money fast. Paying these off should be a key goal.

Mia saw she spent $180/month on gym fees, apps, and TV services she hardly used. Stopping them freed up over $2,000/year—without any change to her daily life.

The Cash Flow Multiplier: The Big Three

Expenses

STOP CARING SO MUCH about coffee, look at the three big spots where you spend up most money:

1. Housing - Rent or home pay should be about 25-30% of what you bring home. If it's more, think about getting a smaller place, letting out a room, or moving.

1. Cars - Owning cars eats up cash. A car that costs $500 a month takes $6,000 a year—cash that you could put into growing your savings. Better to drive good used cars or share rides when needed.

1. Food - Plan your meals, shop smart, and cut back on food from outside. This can help keep a lot of money each month.

Start with any one of these and watch your savings grow big.

Creative Saving Hacks That Work

HERE ARE NEW WAYS YOU can use today:

- The "Work for it" Rule – When you think about buying something, ask: "How many hours do I need to work for this?" If a $200 thing needs 10 work hours, think about whether it's worth it. Most of the time, it's not.

- Cut Your Bills – Once every year, call the firms that give you net, phone, or insurance services. In just 15 minutes, you might cut your bills by $20-$50 each month.

- Get Money Back – Use apps like Rakuten or cards that give you points. But always clear your bill fully. It's only good if you don't pay more later.

The "Wait Three Days" Rule – If you don't need it right away, wait three days before you buy. Many sudden wants will go away, keeping you from buying on a whim.

Case Study: The 50/30/20 Flip

JAMES, WHO MANAGED marketing, used a common money plan: half for needs, 30% for wants, and 20% for savings. Yet, he aimed to stop working by age 45. So, he changed the plan:

Half for saving and growing money

30% for needs

20% for wants

How? He moved to a smaller home, traded his fancy car for an old, better-for-Earth one, and began to plan his meals. In five years, he saved more than $150,000. His "wants" didn't vanish—he just spent more on things like trips and shows, not shopping.

Automate to Win

THE BEST TRICK: SAVE money without seeing it.

- Set up auto moves to savings or investment spots right after you get paid.
- Think of saving as a must-pay bill.

- Keep different accounts to stop spending by mistake.

When Mia made her bank move $800/month to a new account, she soon forgot about it. In one year, she had almost $10,000 tucked away—without feeling held back.

Action Steps: Build Your Saving Engine

1. Check your cash flow – watch all cash for 30 days. You might find a leak.

1. Cut hidden costs – end old subscriptions, talk down bills.

1. Fix one big cost – home, car, or food. Choose the one that saves the most.

1. Set up auto-save 20% (or more) – send it to investments or pay off debt.

1. Use smart tricks – wait 72 hours before buying, stack cashback, and test if it's worth an hour of work to boost results.

The Takeaway

MONEY ISN'T MADE BY just working more—it's made by using what you have smartly. Start with saving. Without it, any extra money from raises or side jobs just slips away. With it, each dollar fights for your freedom.

Mia didn't get rich fast. But by stopping waste, cutting big costs, and making her savings automatic, she gained speed. In a few years, her savings turned to investments, her investments to cash flow, and that cash flow to freedom.

You can do the same—if you start to build your savings motor now.

Chapter 4 — Debt-Free Flight: Cutting Chains That Hold You Back

On a wet Tuesday night, Daniel sat in his car by the food shop, looking at his credit card bill. $18,427. That big number scared him.

He wasn't living big—no big boats, no fancy bags, no wild party times. His debt grew slowly: a doctor bill here, a car fix there, some "I'll clear it next month" costs. Then the extra fees came. Each month, he lost hundreds just to pay the credit card firm.

It felt like going up a hill with heavy chains on his feet. The more he worked, the more he fell back.

But here's what Daniel found out: debt isn't just about money—it locks up your freedom. In debt, you work for others. Your money isn't all yours. Being debt-free isn't just about the figures; it's about breaking free so you can soar.

Debt Is a Wealth Vacuum

LET'S MAKE IT CLEAR: debt stops you from moving forward.

A $5,000 credit card debt with 20% interest takes $1,000 from you every year, just to have that debt.

A $30,000 car loan with 7% interest takes $2,100 from you over five years—plus the car loses value.

Debt keeps you working for others, not for you. Until you break free, true freedom will seem far away.

The Mindset Shift: From Prisoner to Pilot

MANY FEEL BAD ABOUT being in debt, but feeling bad won't fix it—it stops you. Think of it this way: debt isn't forever. It's just a link. And links can be broken.

It's not just about "getting free from debt." It's about setting up a plan that will for sure end your debt. See paying off debt as if you are starting a plane—filling it up, speeding up, then going up—you stop moving slowly and begin to soar.

Plan 1: The Debt Avalanche (Smart Math)

The avalanche way targets the priciest debt first.

1. List all debts by interest rate (high to low).
1. Pay the smallest amounts on all.
1. Put any extra cash into the debt with the highest interest.

Once that's done, move the payment to the next one.

This way, you save more cash in the long run. For instance, Daniel had three debts:

- $8,000 at 19% (credit card)
- $6,000 at 9% (personal loan)
- $4,000 at 4% (car loan)

By paying off the 19% credit card first, he saved over $3,000 in interest versus a random pay method.

Plan 2: The Debt Snowball (Quick Wins)

Math matters, but mind tricks often rule. The snowball way gains speed:

- List debts by size (small to big).
- Hit the smallest first, no matter the interest.
- When one's gone, shift its payment to the next.

Each win boosts your drive. Clearing a $600 store card in one month pushes you to go on.

Plan #3: The Hybrid Engine

Here's a smart trick: mix both. Start with a quick snowball win for energy, then switch to avalanche for top savings. This combo gives you emotional push + math gains.

Cutting Interest: The Silent Multiplier

CUTTING WHAT YOU PAY in interest is much like adding to your pay.

- Balance Transfer Cards – 0% APR for 12–18 months can halt extra costs (if you clear the full amount before high rates start).
- Debt Consolidation Loans - Mix high-rate cards into a single loan with less cost.
- Talk and Bargain - Creditors may cut rates if you just ask, more so if you've paid on time.

Daniel cut his 19% credit card rate to 11% by just making a call. He saved $720 a year right away.

Cash Flow Weapon: The Extra Payment Trick

HERE'S A NEAT TRICK: instead of one payment each month, try making two every two weeks.

- For instance, if you usually pay $400 a month, switch it to $200 every two weeks.

- This way, you make 13 full payments in a year, not just 12, without really feeling it.

- On a big loan like $200,000, this method could help you finish paying off way faster.

Lifestyle Armor: Avoiding the Debt Trap Again

GETTING OUT OF DEBT is just part one—you've to avoid slipping back too.

- Start with an Emergency Fund – Save up $1,000-$2,000 first. This stops every flat tire or doctor's bill from putting you back into debt.

- Stop Buy-Now-Pay-Later Urges – BNPL apps make wants feel like "needs." Get rid of them.

- Use the "Cash-Only Upgrade Rule" – Want a new phone, furniture, or car? Use cash. If you can't, you're not ready to buy it yet.

Case Study: Daniel's Debt-Free Flight

DANIEL USED A MIX OF plans. First, he paid off his $600 store card (snowball), then he hit his 19% card hard (avalanche). He asked for a lower interest rate, changed to pay every two weeks, and put all extra pay into his debt.

In just 26 months, Daniel had no more debt. The $700 each month he used to give to people he owed money to? He moved it to savings and investing. Soon, his "chains" turned into wings.

Action Steps: Build Your Debt-Free Flight Plan

1. Note all debts - Write down how much you owe, the interest rate, and the least you must pay.

1. Choose your plan - Snowball to stay driven, avalanche for better results, or a mix for some of each.

1. Talk to lenders - Try to get lower rates or mix debts wisely.

1. Set auto-pay - Let the bank pull the base amounts, and put any extra money towards debts on purpose.

1. Move saved money - When one debt is gone, do not just keep the extra cash. Use it for the next debt or put it away in savings.

The Takeaway

DEBT IS NOT JUST ABOUT cash—it's about being free. Each dollar you owe ties you down. Each payment you make cuts those ties. When you have no debt, your money is yours again.

Daniel thought it would take a long time to be free from debt. But in truth, it took less than three years. Not because he made more money, but because he made a clear plan.

If you have debt, keep this in mind: you're not stuck—you're just getting ready. Cut the ties, gain speed, and when your last bill is paid, you will feel the rise.

That's when you stop moving slowly on the ground—and start to soar.

Chapter 5 — The Investment Compass: Where to Put Your Money

When Maya got her first big bonus check—$10,000—she did not know what to do with it. Put all in stocks? Buy crypto? Pay off her student loans? Or just keep it in a high-yield savings account until she makes up her mind?

Her pals were no help. One loved day trading, another liked land, and another just said to keep it safe in the bank. Maya was so unsure that she left the cash alone for many months, stuck on what to do.

This is where many folks land: with cash to use but no clear way to use it. With no path, you might freeze like Maya—or worse, rush into bad picks.

The fact? Good use of money is not about running after the next big thing. It's about knowing your spot, where you want to go, and what fits your goals. That's your Money Guide.

The Core Idea: Match Investments to Your Timeline

HERE'S HOW RICH FOLKS use their cash:

- Cash for now (0–3 years): Keep it safe, not big on growth.
- Cash for soon (3–7 years): Mix risk with returns.
- Cash for later (7+ years): Growth wins over safety.

Why? Because the cash you need quickly should stay safe. Think of putting your emergency money in stocks, then seeing it drop 20% right when your car breaks down. That's not smart—that's risky.

Your guide shouldn't be about guessing the market. It's about putting cash in places that fit when you need it.

Short-Term Bucket: The Safety Net

THIS IS THE CASH YOU should not risk losing—money for urgent needs, saving to buy a house soon, or funds for a wedding coming up. You need to keep this money safe and easy to get when needed.

Where to keep it:

- High-Yield Savings Accounts (HYSA): Right now, many banks offer 4–5%. They are backed by the FDIC.
- Certificates of Deposit (CDs): Put away money for 6–12 months to earn a bit more.
- Treasury Bills (T-Bills): They are safe, short-term, and backed by the government.

Action Tip: Set up your urgent fund payments into a different HYSA called "Do Not Touch." Keep it out of your usual view to avoid spending it.

Medium-Term Bucket: Growth with Guardrails

THINK ABOUT A TRIP in 3 years, fixing your house in 5 years, or cash to start a new shop. You need money to grow, but you also want to stay safe from big drops.

Where to keep it:

- Balanced Index Funds (60% stocks and 40% bonds): Usually grow about 6-8% each year and are safer than full stock.

- Real Estate Investment Trusts (REITs): An Easy way to put money in homes with extra cash from dividends.

- Robo-Advisors: They manage money that changes to fit your plans and how much risk you can take.

Quick Tip: Make a "Goal Account" with a robo-advisor (like Wealthfront, Betterment, or another one). Set it for your timeline (like 5 years), and let it handle the risk for you.

Long-Term Bucket: The Growth Engine

THIS IS THE SPOT WHERE you make real money—save for old age, be your boss, leave a big sum for the next ones. The aim: make it grow as much as you can.

Here's where to put it:

- Stock Market (Index Funds & ETFs): The S&P 500 gives you about 10% each year for many years. Wide-market ETFs are key for most rich folks.

- Retirement Accounts (401k, IRA, Roth IRA): Tax breaks make your money grow more. A Roth IRA grows without tax, so what you make, you keep.

- Real Estate: Rent out places, buy and sell homes, or group investments. Real estate not just goes up in value but also gives you steady cash.

- Business Ownership: Owning a business is, over time, the best way to make money. Not stocks or houses—it's businesses. Even a small side job can outdo most markets if it gets big.

Action Tip: Set your money to go into a big ETF (like VTI or VOO) automatically. Even $500 each month, growing at 10% over 30 years, shoots up to nearly $1.1 million.

The Compass Rule: Diversify by Purpose, Not Just Asset

MANY FOLKS BELIEVE that having 20 varied stocks means they are set up with a good mix. Not true. True mix is all about having a clear goal for your funds.

Look here:

- Cash for urgent times → HYSA (safe)
- Cash saved for a home in 5 years → Mixed set of items (grow and stay steady)
- Cash for old age times → Funds with stocks + Property (grow over years)

Give each dollar a task. Don't let the money for the house do the work meant for your old age money—or the other way.

Clever Strategy: The Barbell Portfolio

HERE'S A TRICK FROM smart money folks: divide cash into super-safe and big-growth, leave out the in-between.

- 80% in safe stuff (like savings accounts, government bonds).
- 20% in things that can grow a lot (like shares, digital money, new businesses).

By doing this, the safe part keeps you safe, and the growth part could make big money. It's a way to play it smart with risk: you can only lose so much, but you can gain a lot.

Avoiding Compass Errors: What Not to Do

- Stay away from the hype. Meme stocks, cheap cryptos, and "hot tips" on social media often take more money than they make.

- Keep it simple. If you can't make a 12-year-old get your investment, maybe you shouldn't go for it.

- Only use what you can lose. Never use the cash meant for rent, bills, or food in the market.

Case Study: Maya's Compass

AYA SET UP HER BONUS like this:

- $2,000 into a HYSA for a safe back-up.

- $3,000 into a Balanced Index Fund for future trips.

- $5,000 into a Roth IRA for growing long-term.

A year on, instead of just watching a still checking account, she saw her cash at work in three ways. Even more, she knew what her money was doing.

Action Steps: Build Your Compass Today

1. Set your goals by time. Short-range (0–3 years), mid-range (3–7 years), long-range (7+ years).

1. Group your cash. Every dollar should have a job.

1. Choose the best tools. Use a high-yield savings account for short-term needs, mixed funds for middle years, and stocks or property for long-term terms.

1. Make it automatic. Don't rely on your will.

1. Check each year. Change things as your aims or plans change.

The Takeaway

PUTTING MONEY DOWN isn't just about spotting the next big hit like Tesla or Bitcoin. It's more about making a plan that points your cash towards your aims.

Maya's key move wasn't picking ETFs over crypto, but knowing that every buck must have a plan. Once you fix your guide, you won't drift without aim. Rather, your cash will move you slowly towards freedom, safety, and getting bigger.

Chapter 6 — The 80/20 Wealth Rule: High-Impact Money Moves

When Ethan began dealing with money, he saw it like dirty clothes: all over and too much. He cut out coupons, skipped his morning drink, and spent ages looking at small changes in card rewards. But after a year, his money grew just a little.

Then, one day, a wise person told him, "Ethan, most of what you gain comes from a few of your acts. Don't fold socks when you should be doing big things."

That was his big wake-up. Ethan saw he was stuck on small change while missing the big steps that could change his money life. In two years, he wasn't just keeping money — he was making it grow.

This is the 80/20 Money Rule at work. It's about where to look. Not all money actions are big. Some start waves that change your money world; some you don't notice. The trick to making more money fast isn't doing it all—it's doing the things that count the most.

The Core Idea: Small Inputs, Big Outputs

THE 80/20 RULE, OR the Pareto Principle, means that most of the time, 80% of what we get comes from just 20% of what we do. When we talk about money:

. A few big choices—such as where we live, our debt, and what we invest in—shape most of our money life.

. The small stuff—like making your almond milk at home—doesn't change much.

The risk is spending too much time on small money tasks and missing the big, important moves.

High-Impact Money Moves

HERE ARE THE KEY 20% moves that lead to 80% (or more) of your results.

1. Housing: Your Top Tool

For most, housing is the biggest cost. Living slightly below what you make can build wealth faster than not buying small things like coffee.

- Plan: Keep housing costs under 25–30% of what you take home.

- Trick: Try "house hacking"—rent out a spare room or buy a duplex and rent out half. Even $500 a month in rent helps a lot. That's $6,000 a year—more than what most save.

2. Income: Make the Gap Bigger

You can't just budget your way to more money if your pay doesn't increase. Small raises are not enough—use skills and chances that double or triple what you earn.

- Plan: Focus on skills that are worth a lot (like sales, coding, design, managing projects).

- Trick: Use the "$10k Test." Ask if this skill, chance, or project will add at least $10,000 to your pay in 12–18 months? If yes, it's worth your time.

3. Debt: Break the Chains

Interest costs you money. High-interest debt can eat up more money than many years of saving.

- Plan: Go after high-interest debts (>8%) hard.

- Trick: Use Debt Avalanche + Side Hustle. Put all extra money (plus money from side jobs) towards the debt with the highest interest. Once it's gone, move to the next.

4. Automation: Set It and Forget It

Having to decide all the time can lose you money. If you set things to do on their own, your system will make money even when you sleep.

- Plan: Set up automatic money moves into investment accounts right after payday.

- Trick: Build a Wealth Ladder:

  - Step 1: Send 10% automatically to an emergency fund.

  - Step 2: Put 15% into retirement automatically.

  - Step 3: Any extra goes to a taxable investment or side job fund.

5. Investing: Simple is Better

You don't need tons of accounts or special assets. One or two good investment choices, used all the time, can do a lot.

. Plan: Choose broad index funds (like VTI, VOO, or global ETFs).

. Trick: Use the "Rule of 72." Divide 72 by your expected return to see how fast your money doubles. With 10% growth, your money doubles about every 7 years.

6. Taxes: The Quiet Loss

Many wait till April to think about taxes, but they take a big part of what you earn. Setting up your money in a tax-smart way helps your wealth grow quietly.

. Plan: Use all the tax-help accounts (401k, Roth IRA, HSA).

. Trick: If self-employed, set up an S-Corp or Solo 401k to save a lot on taxes each year. That's money growing for you, not going to the IRS.

The 80/20 Audit: Find Your Power Moves

LET'S TRY THIS EASY task:

1. List your five main costs.
1. List your three main ways to make money.
1. Mark the biggest one in each list.

This is where you should work smart. For many people, this could mean changing where they live or trying to earn more money, not worrying too much about saving a small amount on food shopping.

Case Study: Ethan's Shift

ETHAN GAVE UP HUNTING for coupons and changed gears:

- He moved to a small flat, which cut his costs by $600 each month.

- He learned a new job skill in digital marketing, which increased his yearly income by $25,000.
- He set his money to auto-invest in index funds.

In just one year, he put away $7,200 on housing, made $25,000 extra, and put 20% of his pay into investments. That's a boost of $32,200—way more than what he saved by cutting small costs.

Action Steps: Apply the 80/20 Wealth Rule

1. Check what's key in spending and earning. See what brings in the most cash or goes out the most.

1. Choose one strong move. Don't try to do too much—start with what gives you the most in return.

1. Set up automatic money steps. Ease the load of choosing; this way, it gets done for you.

1. Pay no heed to clutter. Skip the tricks that don't help.

1. Look back each year. When you make more money, adjust where your main effort needs to go.

The Takeaway

MONEY DOES NOT GROW by getting all things right. It grows by doing the right things over and over. The 80/20 Money Rule is clear: put your work where it grows, not where it fades.

Stop fixing small money issues. Start making big changes.

Chapter 7 — Real Estate Freedom: Owning Assets That Pay You

When Sarah got her first home, she felt she was living the "American Dream" - a white fence, yard parties, and paying the home loan each month. But years later, she saw a harsh truth: the house wasn't making her more money; it was just making her tired. With property tax, upkeep, and loan payments, her home seemed more like a money hole than a help.

Then she ran into Chris, an old work friend who quit work at 42. He didn't strike rich from tech or win the lotto. He had property, but not like Sarah's. While she paid for her home each month, Chris had places that paid him back. Rent money came steadily, and these places got worth more as time went on.

This is the core of Real Estate Freedom: having things that don't just look nice but also bring cash in every month. Done well, real estate isn't about just blocks and earth—it's about making a system where cash from others helps you be free of money worries.

The Core Idea: Cash-Flow First, Appreciation Second

MANY THINK MAKING MONEY in real estate is all about getting a house for a low price, waiting for its value to go up, and selling it for more. That's just guessing, not true investing.

Real freedom in real estate comes from having cash flow—places that make money now, not just in the future. Rising value is just a bonus, not the main thing.

The aim is easy: have properties where the rent pays for everything (loan, taxes, insurance, upkeep) and still gives you some extra cash. This extra cash flow is what can get you to retire early.

How to Spot a Freedom Property

NOT ALL HOMES ARE THE same. A bright, new flat in a cool city may seem great on Instagram, but it may take all your cash in real life.

Here is what you should aim for:

1. The 1% Rule – Monthly rent needs to be at least 1% of the buy cost.

○ For example, if you get a home for $150,000, try for at least $1,500 a month in rent.

○ This quick check stops you from going after homes that look great but do not pay off.

2. Low Run Costs – Stay away from cash holes. Old houses with many fixes can ruin gains. Pick homes with good roofs, new systems, and small fix needs.

3. Growing Areas, Not Just Hot Ones – The top spots are often not-too-big towns with job growth, cheap homes, and more people coming—not costly beach towns where the math often fails.

Unique Wealth-Building Strategies

HERE ARE WAYS YOU CAN start now, if you have $5,000 or $500,000:

1. House Hacking

- Stay in one part, let out the rest. This is how many start.
- Get a duplex, triplex, or fourplex.
- Stay in one place, let the others out.

Your renters pay your loan while you live almost free.

For example, Sarah sold her big home and got a fourplex. She stayed in one place while the rest paid off her loan. In two years, her costs fell to almost nothing, and she began to save more money.

2. Short-Term Rentals

Sites like Airbnb can make a side room or holiday home into a money maker.

- Look for places with tourists, big events, or hospitals (nurses may need short-term stays).
- Make cleaning and check-in easy with automated help.
- Keep an eye on city laws—some places stop or cap short-term lets.

Tip: Aim for "dull" cities with steady needs (near schools or hospitals) over tourist-packed spots.

3. Real Estate Partnerships

You don't have to do it alone.

- Join up with someone who has what you lack (money, know-how, or access to properties).

- Use joint plans where you split gains and cash flow.

This can speed up your entry while you share both ups and downs.

4. REITs and Split Investing

Not set to buy a place? Real Estate Trusts (REITs) or split sites let you own parts of places that earn money without the need to deal with upkeep or renters.

- Public REITs (like VNQ) work like stocks.
- Split sites let you put $500–$1,000 in big property deals.

It's less direct, but it's a good first step.

The Math That Matters

BEFORE YOU SPEND, TRY this easy math:

Cash Flow = Rent - (Mortgage + Taxes + Insurance + Fixing + Empty space)

If this leaves you with good extra cash, you're doing well.

Hint: Always think there will be 5–10% empty times and 5–10% fix costs. Numbers that work only when things go just right will fall apart in real life.

Real-Life Example: Chris's Path

CHRIS BEGAN WITH $20,000. He:

. Purchased a two-unit house for $120,000.

. Paid $20,000 upfront and took a loan for the balance.

. Rented each place for $750, so he made $1,500 each month.

After costs, he kept $300 each month. Not a big deal at first. But he put that money into another place. Skip ahead 10 years: he had 15 units making more than $8,000 each month, clear. That's cash for real freedom.

Action Steps: Your First Property Playbook

1 KNOW YOUR AREA. TAKE 30 days to look at places to rent on Zillow, Craigslist, or Apartments.com. Check rent-to-price numbers.

2 Do the math. Use the 1% Rule as a guide, then add up real cash flow with all costs.

3 Begin tiny. A duplex or even a basement flat can start your journey.

4 Use loans wisely. Fixed-rate loans keep your pay small while rents go up.

5 Put money back in. Use the cash from the first place to buy the second, then the third. Keep going until your holdings pay for your way of life.

The Takeaway

OWNING A BIG HOUSE does not set you free in real estate. It's about having the right places—houses, flats, or shops—that bring in money. Every rent you get is not just money—it shows that what you own does the hard work for you.

Put money flow first, growth next, and keep putting money back in. Soon, you will have a bunch of places that do more than cover costs—they give you your time back.

Why? Because the big dream isn't just a house with a neat fence. The true dream is to never have to wake up to an alarm again.

Chapter 8 — The Side Hustle Accelerator: From Extra Cash to True Wealth

On a wet Tuesday night, Michael was in his car, not far from work. Yet another long day. Another meal not shared with his kids. He wasn't sad—his work paid well—but he felt trapped.

He was looking at his phone when he saw a pal selling clip art online. "This can't be good cash," he thought. Just to know more, he messaged her. She replied with a smile. "I got $800 this month—easy as that."

That sparked something in Michael. He didn't quit or jump without thinking. He just tried out a small side job. In half a year, his little money-making side thing was bringing in $1,200 a month. Two years on, it earned more than his main job. What began as spare change turned into his way to be rich.

This is what the Side Hustle Accelerator does—turns some extra cash into real wealth. It isn't only about making more money. It's about making that extra cash grow and build up fast.

The Core Idea: Don't Just Hustle—Accelerate

MANY THINK THAT SIDE jobs are just quick fixes: drive Uber for gas cash, bring food for house money, teach web for more bucks. That's fine—but if you end there, you'll keep running in place.

The big change comes when you use side job money for investing.

See it like this: your main job covers day-to-day life. Your side job gets you ahead.

Rather than using that extra $500 or $1,000 on tech or fun nights, put it into big money moves—investing, starting a business, or paying off debt that grows over time.

STEP 1: PICK A SIDE Job with Big Payoff

Not all side gigs pay the same. Some pull you in for more hours just for more cash (like gig driving). Others give big results for little work: you put in a bit now and get a lot back later.

Great Side Jobs:

. Digital Goods - eBooks, templates, online classes. Make once, sell over and over.

. Skills for Hire - Writing, design, coding. First, swap time for cash, then grow to a business or product.

. Making Content - YouTube, podcasts, blogs. Starts slow, big gains later.

. Buying/Selling - Books, collectibles, furniture. Costs little to start, grows with smart steps.

Go for what suits your skills and drive. The real win is extra cash that keeps growing.

Step 2: Test Time with 80/20 Rule

Your side job should grow your time, not eat it up. Ask:

. "Which small tasks make most of the money?"

. Focus on those. Either make the rest easy or stop them.

For example, if selling used books, find good ones to sell most of the time, and don't spend ages fixing online posts. If freelancing, go for big-pay clients, not little $20 jobs.

Step 3: Turn Job Money into Real Wealth

Here's where some miss the boat. They get side cash, then blow it.

Set up a Side Job Wealth Funnel instead:

1. First $1,000/month → Clear bad debt (credit cards, high loans). Each $100 debt gone = more cash to use.

2. Next $1,000/month → Save for rainy days (3–6 months' costs). This keeps panic at bay.

3. After that → Put money in things that grow:

○ Simple stock funds.

○ Putting money down on a house (property that makes you money).

○ Pour back into your business (add help, make things run smoothly, grow).

Key idea: see side job cash as "can't touch growth cash." Don't spend it like normal cash until it builds wealth.

Real Story: Lisa's Digital Empire

Lisa, a teacher, started by making and selling lesson templates on TeachersPayTeachers. At first, she earned $50/month. Rather than spend this, she saved until she had $500, then bought better design tools and hired help.

In two years, she made $4,000/month without much work. She used that cash for a rental house. Now, her side job pays more than teaching—it's also got her an asset that grows in value.

Her trick? Putting the side cash back into her side job.

Step 4: Make Systems, Not More Work

The risk of side gigs is burning out. The way out is systems.

- Make things run themselves: Use tools like Zapier or Canva, or apps to plan things.
- Get help: Pay others for repeating tasks (making lists, fixing up, helping customers).
- Turn your service into a thing you sell (a designer goes from working for each client to selling design sets).

Aim to make the side job work with you doing less and less.

Step 5: Think Long, Not Short

Side gigs may seem small in the first year. But over ten years, they can grow massive.

Check the math:

- $1,000/month from a side gig = $12,000/year.
- At 8% growth for 10 years = over $180,000.
- Keep putting it back in, and your "extra cash" turns into a big stack—even more with growth.

That's why side gigs aren't just for extra dollars. They are to build wealth fast.

Action Steps: Launching Your Accelerator

1 LOOK AT WHAT YOU can do and like. Choose one side hustle that stands out.

2 Plan a quick three-month push. Aim to prove it works and make your first $500.

3 Start a new bank account. Put all money from the hustle there—never use it for daily buys.

4 Make a plan to put money back. Choose now: debt to savings, to things you own. Follow it.

5 Make it automatic. When you start to earn all the time, use time or cash to grow without much work.

The Takeaway

SIDE JOBS ARE NOT JUST small gigs now—they make you rich fast. The line between some cash and real wealth is in how you work with the cash.

Michael made more than $1,200 a month; he used it to buy things that let him live free. Lisa did not just sell plans; she made a way to get a house she can rent out.

You don't need to leave your job at once. But if you start now—pick a good side job, use your money smart, and make plans—you'll soon see that your side job is not just some "extra." It gets you to be free with money.

The key win is not just more work. It's getting your money to work more, while you get to enjoy life how you want.

Chapter 9 — The Tax Advantage Playbook

When Sarah got her first big job promotion, she was so happy—until tax time came. Her pay went up by $15,000, but after all the taxes, she felt she got less than half. "I worked so hard, and it's like the government got my raise," she told her friend while they had coffee, half-joking but also sad.

Her friend leaned in and shared a tip that changed everything:

"Rich folks don't hate taxes. They just know the tricks. You're playing a simple game. They're playing a smart game."

That night, Sarah jumped into learning about tax tricks. In one year, by picking smart moves—nothing bad, nothing wild—she cut her tax cost by over $9,000. That wasn't just a tax return. That was her own money she kept each year. And she learned something big:

How you make money is key, but how you keep it is even more key.

The Core Idea: Taxes Are Your Largest Expense

MANY THINK THEIR HOME pay is their main cost. That's not true. For many who make money, taxes eat up the most—federal, state, local, land, sales, and payroll.

Rich folks don't just make more; they save more. They set up their money world to use tax rules well. The key to the Tax Advantage Playbook is this: not dodging, not tricks, but setting your cash to fit the system rules so you lose less.

Step 1: Change Earned Income to Less-Taxed Income

Your regular job's salary (W-2 income) gets taxed a lot. You pay taxes before you get your money. Yet, money from a business, investments, and houses often gets taxed less, or not at all.

Example:

- $100,000 salary → taxes up to 37% plus other taxes.
- $100,000 in long-term money from selling things → taxes from 0% to 20%.

Don't quit your job now. Work on making money from side jobs, investing, or owning places that don't get taxed as much.

Step 2: Get Business Owner Perks

A small side job can bring big tax cuts. The state helps business start-ups by letting you cut costs like your home office, your net, and your phone.

What you can do:

- Cut costs on part of your home office, net, and phone.
- Cut travel costs if it's for business.
- Cut costs on gear, programs, and learning for your job.

Sarah made her craft store an LLC. Now, her old laptop and phone costs count as business expenses. Her trips to fairs are also counted as costs. She's not just spending; she's shifting personal expenses into business costs as allowed.

Step 3: Use Retirement Funds as Secret Tax Tools

Retirement funds not only save for later—they cut taxes now.

• 401(k)/403(b): Putting money in lowers your taxes now. Free money from your employer.

• Roth IRA/Roth 401(k): Pay taxes now, don't pay on growth later. Good if taxes might go up later.

• SEP IRA/Solo 401(k): For side hustlers or small business folk, it lets you save more without taxes.

Top tip: Use a Roth for money you won't need for a long time, and traditional accounts when you're making the most money.

Step 4: Houses Give Tax Benefits

Owning real estate comes with three big perks:

1. Letting you cut costs on paper for wear and tear, lowering taxes, but keeping income high.

1. Swapping properties without taxes using a 1031 Exchange.

1. If you sell your main house after living in it for two years, no tax on gains up to $250,000 (or $500,000 for couples).

Example: Mark got a rental place. It earned him $400 a month after costs. He showed a loss with depreciation, so he paid less in taxes. More cash in hand with a smaller tax bill.

Step 5: Accounts That Grow Free From Taxes

Some accounts let your money grow without ever being taxed again:

• Health Savings Account: Tax cuts when putting money in, no taxes as it grows, and no taxes when used for health.

- 529 Plans: No taxes on the money that grows, used for school costs.

- Life Insurance: Some make use of certain policies as ways to grow money without taxes.

Think of these as safe places in your money plan—spaces where your cash grows safe from taxes.

Step 6: Timing Matters in Taxes

Saving on taxes isn't only about what you make, but when.

- Sell something you've invested in after a year → pay less in capital gains taxes.

- Sell sooner → pay more as regular income.

- Group deductions in a year to use them fully, then go simple the next.

Small changes in when you do things can save a lot.

Step 7: Get a Tax Team Early

Rich folks don't handle taxes alone. They have tax experts like CPAs who save them a lot in the long run.

A must-do: Even if you're starting small, have a yearly "tax strategy talk" with an expert. Not just during tax time in April. Ask:

- "How can I cut next year's taxes?"

- "Which business form is best for being flexible?"

The Takeaway: Taxes Aren't a Penalty, They're a

Game

SARAH DID NOT GET RICH fast. But by using the Tax Advantage Guide—changing kinds of income, using retirement and real estate plans, and putting her tax savings back in—she kept close to $100,000 more over ten years than she would have without it.

That is cash that bought her first real estate to invest in. That is cash growing for her future.

Taxes are not just a once-a-year thing. They are a life game. And if you know the rules, you stop playing simple games while others play smart ones.

The fact is clear: You don't need to make more to have more. You need to hold on to more of what you make. And with the guide in your hands, you can do that.

Chapter 10 — The Minimalist Millionaire: Spending With Purpose

When Marcus got his year-end bonus, he did what many folks do—he had fun. He got the latest phone, a better TV, and a fancy watch. For weeks, all felt great. But by spring, he was in the same spot: working a lot, paying off cards, and asking why he was never ahead.

Then he met Clara. She made less than Marcus, had a small flat, and drove an old car. But she had zero debt. She went on trips three times a year, put a lot into savings, and planned to retire early, before 45.

"How can you do this?" Marcus asked.

Clara smiled.

"I don't just spend less, I spend with a plan."

The Core Idea: Money Is a Tool, Not a Trophy

THE MINIMALIST MILLIONAIRE way isn't about going without or just eating cheap food. It's about seeing that every buck you use has a job - either to add real value to your life or to just fade away.

Most folk just buy things as they come. Ads, what's hot, and what friends do push how they use money. But minimalist millionaires think about each buy, matching it to what really counts - freedom, self-growth, and happiness.

The key is not how much money you make. It's about how much real use each buck holds.

Step 1: Check the Noise

You need to see where your cash flows before you can use it well. Keep an eye on every buy for one month—not just the big things, but each coffee, sign-up, and quick buy.

Ask yourself:

- Did this buy add long-term worth?
- Could I have had a good life without it?
- Did it match my aims—or was it just good ads?

Do this now: Mark the top five "waste zones" in your buys. For Marcus, it was ordering food, too many subs, and fast tech buys. Clara didn't say "never treat yourself." She said, "Cut the noise, boost the music."

Step 2: Set Your "Money Guide"

Clara had an easy rule for each buy: Does this help me reach my dream life?

She picked having fun over owning things, feeling free over looking rich, and knowing more over fancy stuff. Her guide was not about being cheap—it was about being sure.

Your guide might be:

- Stopping work early.
- Paying for travel.
- Making wealth for the family.
- Getting more free time.

Every buy should help your guide or at least not hurt it.

Step 3: The Better Rule

Rich folk with few needs don't hold back forever. They pick better when needed.

Rule: Only get better in things you use a lot or love.

- What shoes do you wear all the time? Good to buy comfy ones.
- Bed, do you sleep for 8 hours? Needed.
- Tools for daily cooking? Wise.

But an expensive couch you hardly use? More cars when you stay home? That's not better—it's just dead weight.

Do this now: Write down the "Top 5 Life Boosts" you use all day. They are worth the big spend. Keep the rest low.

Step 4: Wait on Wants

Fast buys can mess up big dreams. The rich minimalist uses time as a check.

Try the 30-Day Rule:

- See something you like.
- Write it down.
- Wait 30 days.
- If you still want it—and it fits your guide—get it.

Often, you'll find the want fades. What's left is sureness.

Step 5: Move the Extra

When you spend right, you save more. But don't let that extra cash get lost in random buys; put it to work right away.

For Clara, every saved dollar went right into three parts:

1. Investing – stocks, funds, and houses.

1. Learning – books, classes, and talks.

1. Having fun – travel and friends.

By moving savings with purpose, she changed "cutting back" into "moving up."

Step 6: Make Your Values Automatic

It's hard to keep on track if each buy needs hard choices. The rich minimalist sets up systems.

- Set auto money moves to investments on payday.
- End auto subs you hardly use.
- Use cash boxes or separate accounts for extra spending.

Auto makes hardship the norm.

Step 7: Try the Minimal Mind

Less isn't the same for all. For some, it's fewer things. For others, it's more free days. For many, it's choosing what matters in friends, plans, and even what you hear online.

Cash is just part of it. By making all simpler—fewer things, fewer pulls—you make space for aim and freedom.

Real-Life Example: Clara's $100,000 Shift

FOR FIVE YEARS, CLARA moved only $1,500 each month from waste to goals:

- $1,000 into index funds.
- $300 to travel.
- $200 for classes.

That $1,000 every month grew to more than $80,000. The trips gave her lasting memories. The classes upped her pay by 20%.

She didn't cut back more. She just spent time with a plan.

The Takeaway: Wealth Is What You Keep, Joy Is What You Choose

OVER TIME, MARCUS TOOK up Clara's way. He kept loving life—but cut out needless buys. He saw that with less stuff, he felt freer.

Rich minimalists aren't tight with cash. They plan well. They know that each buck can make or break your future.

The trick isn't to cut back, but to use money with intent.

When you mix cash with what matters to you, you don't just build wealth. You boost freedom, happiness, and a life free from what doesn't count.

Chapter 11 — The Global Wealth Strategy: Thinking Beyond Borders

When Nadia's work cut her off in her hometown in Ohio, she had to make a tough call. Her friends looked for jobs in a dying field. But Nadia had a new plan. She saw that many wanted to learn English online from faraway places. She began to teach kids in South Korea, then Japan, then Turkey. In one year, she didn't just earn more cash than before—she got paid in three types of money, flew to see her kids, and put cash in plans overseas.

Her friends thought she got lucky. But Nadia knew it wasn't luck—she was all over the map.

The Core Idea: Don't Play the Game on One Board

MANY FOLKS MAKE MONEY inside one country. They work in one place, get paid in one type of money, and put their cash in one market. It's like only using half the chessboard—you miss out on moves that could turn it all around.

Global wealth plans mean mixing up your life from place to place—work, money, and even where you live. Why? Because when one place trips up, another gets ahead. When one money type drops, another climbs. And when one market shuts, another starts up.

The point isn't to leave your homeland. It's to grow your choices.

Step 1: Make Money in Different Currencies

Think of money as air. If you only get air from one place and it runs out, you're in a bad spot. But if you get air from many places, you can go anywhere.

What to do:

- Remote Work: Work from anywhere—do jobs like writing, advising, creating, or coding. Sites like Upwork or Fiverr let you make money in dollars even if you aren't in the US.

- Geo-Arbitrage: Stay in a cheap place but make money in a strong money type. For example, make US dollars while you live in Mexico, Portugal, or Thailand.

- Digital Products: Sell courses, books, or apps in dollars, euros, or pounds.

Example: A designer in Manila earns $60 per job from US clients. At home, that job pays $8. By making dollars and spending pesos, he gains more.

Step 2: Put Money in Places Outside Your Home

Many people only put money in their own country's market. That's risky. You wouldn't put all your money in one firm, right? But many do that with their own country.

Choices:

- Global Funds & ETFs: A simple way to connect to markets in Europe, Asia, and other growing areas.

- Property Outside: In some places, you can buy properties to let out for much less than in the US or Europe. Think about flats in Eastern Europe or South America, which cost less but earn a lot.

- Worldwide Stocks That Pay: Firms like Nestlé in Switzerland or Toyota in Japan make money all over. This guards against local low points.

Smart move: Aim to have 20-30% of your money in places outside your own country.

Step 3: Plan for a "Plan B" Home

What if your country has big troubles, like political fights, tax raises, or money crashes? Do you have a backup? Some rich minimalists do—via second homes or even new citizenships.

Ways to start:

- Home by Money: Some places let you stay if you put money into houses or local firms. Portugal, Greece, and Panama are known for this.

- Visas for Work or School: Teaching, learning, or working from afar can lead to new chances.

- Visas for Long-Stay Remote Work: Spots like Estonia, Croatia, and Costa Rica welcome those who work from home to stay longer.

You don't have to move right away—but having a second home option is like having money in a safe.

Step 4: Use the "Global Tax Break"

Tax rules are very different around. In some places, money made outside is hardly taxed or not at all. Some even have tax perks for new people.

Example: Portugal lets certain workers pay fewer taxes for 10 years through their NHR program. Dubai and Monaco charge no income tax. Panama does not tax money made outside if you live there.

Smart move: Look into one place with low taxes that suits you. Even if you don't go there now, knowing your choices can guide your future.

Step 5: Think About Place, Not Just Money

Being rich globally isn't just about money types and where to put your money. It's about living where your cash, time, and work are worth the most.

- Cost Edge: Living in a city where $2,000 a month feels rich.
- Life Quality: Having good health care, schools, and safety often beats the richest places.
- Life From Money: Beaches in Bali, cafes in Lisbon, or mountains in Colombia—all for much less than you'd pay in the US or UK.

Real Talk: The Global Triangle

One person I know uses a "Global Triangle Strategy":

- Made in the US (clients pay in dollars).
- Put money in Eastern Europe (big rents, low costs).
- Live in South America (cheap living, good life quality).

By spreading his plan over three places, he made his wealth grow three times faster—without tripling his work.

Step 6: Begin Small, Think Big

You don't need to move right now. Start growing your global wealth bit by bit:

1. Open a multi-money account (like Wise or Revolut).
1. Put one global ETF in your choices.
1. Look at the property market abroad online.
1. Try to earn money from abroad—find one client outside.
1. Check out one place where you might get residency.

Each step grows your options.

The Takeaway: Wealth Without Borders

NADIA GOT RICH NOT by making more money than others, but by making a life that stood strong no matter the changes in one place.

Having money all around the world isn't about turning away from home—it's about making a big safety net that lets you do well anywhere.

When you look past your land, being rich is not just about having cash or things. It's about having choices. In the race to be free with money, choices are the best thing to have.

Chapter 12 — Risk-Proofing Your Plan

In 2008, Marcus felt he could not be beaten. He ran a good business, owned a house that grew in value fast, and had lots of bank stocks. Then the big money crash came. His clients left, his stocks fell hard, and his house was worth less than what he owed on it. In just one night, Marcus went from the top of the world to just trying to keep the lights on.

Years after, when things got better, Marcus told me something I won't forget: "I wasn't just not ready. I was weak. I set up everything, thinking only good would happen. When the bad came, I had no way to fight it."

This is where most of us mess up. We make money plans that only work if all goes as we think it will. But money that isn't safe from risk isn't money—it's just luck that will soon be gone.

The Core Idea: Build a Plan That Survives Storms

RISK-PROOFING ISN'T about running from risk. Risk is a part of life and chance. It's about seeing what might go bad and setting up guards so that one bad thing doesn't ruin all your work.

Think of it like making a ship: you can't make the sea calm, but you can make your ship strong so it won't go down in the first big wave.

Step 1: Ask "What If?"

Start by asking: What could mess up my plan?

List out all risks in three groups:

- Personal: Losing jobs, health issues, family problems.

- Money: Stock market crash, high inflation, economic downturn.

- World: Disease spread, wars, natural disasters, unstable politics.

Example: If 80% of your money comes from one job, that's a big risk. If all your cash is in one stock market, that's a risk too.

Action tip: Note down five "what ifs" that could stop your plans. Knowing these is the first step to staying safe.

Step 2: Make Money Safety Nets

Like cars need systems to handle road bumps, your money plan needs safety nets.

- Emergency Fund 2.0: Save for more than 3-6 months. Figure out how long you can last without money. Try to save for at least 12 months of basic costs in cash or similar things.

- Several Ways to Make Money: Don't depend on one paycheck. Even a small side job (online teaching, freelance work, renting out property) can help during bad times.

- Spread Your Investments: Put your money in different things (stocks, bonds, real estate, cash), places (home and away), and fields (tech, health, energy).

Real story: In 2020, freelancers who only worked on events or travel lost jobs in a day. Those with more ways to make money, even small ones like selling online goods, managed to stay ok.

Step 3: Insurance Is Crucial

Insurance might seem dull, but it's key to keeping wealth safe. Rich folks don't just ignore insurance—they get more, but wisely.

- Health Insurance: A health issue can eat up years of savings.

- Disability Insurance: What if you can't work for a year?

- Life Insurance: It helps your family if you're not around. (Hint: term life usually gives good coverage for less money.)

- Umbrella Policies: Cheap coverage that adds safety for home, car, or business risks.

Action tip: Check your insurance yearly. Ask: If the worst happened, would I still have money?

Step 4: Stay Safe From Inflation and Money Changes

People usually think of money as unchanging. But your money loses value each year due to inflation. Worse, if you live worldwide or plan to retire in another country, changes in money value can hit hard.

- Inflation Shields: Hold things that gain value with inflation—real estate, strong company stocks, or bonds tied to inflation.

- Diversify Currencies: Keep savings or investments in several currencies. Tools like Wise, Revolut, or multi-currency accounts help.

Case study: In Argentina, middle-class families who only had money in pesos lost almost everything when inflation soared. Those who saved some in U.S. dollars kept their buying power.

Step 5: Test Your Money Plan

Pilots train with failed engines in simulators. Investors should, too.

Try this: Pretend your net worth drops by 40% tomorrow. What would happen?

- Could you still pay bills?
- Would you sell your investments in panic?
- Do you have enough spread out to bounce back?

Use tools like online retirement calculators, but test for tough times—higher inflation, lower gains, or late income. If your plan stands, you've built a strong defense.

Step 6: Be Ready to Change

Avoiding risks isn't just about money—it's about how we act. The biggest danger isn't always the market; we struggle to change if needed.

- Keep Fixed Costs Low: The less you need for your daily life, the quicker you can change if life shifts.
- Learn Many Skills: Keep learning new skills that work in various job areas. (Example: a marketer who learns data analysis can switch jobs faster than one who only knows about ads.)
- Think About Your Location: Where you live matters. Being able to move to a cheaper place, even for a while, can be a big safety net.

Step 7: Have a "Plan Z"

Always have a backup plan. Entrepreneurs like Jeff Bezos call this "Plan Z"—the option when everything else fails.

For you, that could mean:

- Moving back with family for a while.
- Moving to a cheaper country where your savings last longer.
- Taking a stable but simpler job to pay the bills while you start over.

The twist? People with a Plan Z often don't need it—because just having it makes them more sure to keep going.

The Takeaway: Antifragile Wealth

MARCUS FOUND OUT THE tough way that a weak plan is like a big house on sand. It looks great until the water comes in.

Keeping your money safe isn't about being scared—it's about being free. It means not spending nights wide awake, worried about the next day, and instead resting well, knowing you've set up strong shields to handle any big winds or rains.

At the end, real wealth isn't just about how much you make when things are good—it's about how much you hold on to when hard times surely hit.

Chapter 13 — Automation: Putting Wealth on Autopilot

Each January, Lisa made a plan: "This year, I'll save more." But by each December, she'd look at her bank stuff and ask, "Where did all the money go?" She made good money, but daily life—surprise bills, eating out, buying stuff online—ate up all her good plans.

Then she did something new. She did not just try harder, she made a new way: her work pay sent some money right to savings, her money bits got bought each month on their own, and her bills were paid by themselves. A year later, Lisa had more saved up than in the last five years—all without a big change in how she lived.

It wasn't about trying harder. It was about making it automatic.

The Core Idea: Systems Beat Discipline

A LOT OF FOLKS LOSE money not because they don't know the right moves, but because they can't keep it up all the time. Drive runs low, sudden needs come up, and the easy way wins. Setting up auto-pay takes the need for strong will out of it by making smart money moves automatic.

See it like a moving belt for your cash. After it's ready, your cash goes where it must, no matter if you're watching or not.

Step 1: Set Your Savings on Auto

When money first lands in your account, it's as if it is already gone—you just don't know where yet. Change the order you deal with your money.

- Save First: Make a plan so part of your money (10–20% if you can) goes right into savings or funds before you even see it.

- Use Different Pots: Make special accounts for each plan—you need one for emergencies, one for travel, and one for buying a house. Giving names to these accounts puts your money to work and keeps you from taking it out.

- The "Out of Sight Rule": Once you move your money, make taking it back hard. Don't join your savings to the card you use every day.

Real-life story: A teacher I know opened three accounts—one for a house, one for trips, and one for urgent needs. Each time she got paid, her money was split into these. She said it was like "planting trees that grew alone while she taught."

Step 2: Set Your Investing to Auto

Markets can rise or fall—and trying to catch the right moment often fails. Auto-investing helps you avoid the drama.

- Regular Buy-In: Put in a set amount often (every week or month), no matter the market look. This way, you end up buying more when costs are low and less when high.

- Target Funds or ETFs: Just set these up and then forget about them. They adjust on their own as you get nearer to stopping work.

- Auto-Advice: Use platforms like Betterment or Wealthfront to manage and adjust your funds for you.

Tip: The top error investors make is not making bad choices—it's just stopping. Auto-investing makes sure you keep going, even if the news is scary.

Step 3: Stay Aware While Paying Bills on Auto

Late fees are like fines for not being sorted. Auto payments fix this—if handled wisely.

- Regular Bills: Auto-pay your day-to-day bills like lights, internet, and tiny bits on cards to avoid missing them.

- Check Often: Once a month, look at your bills for odd costs. Using auto doesn't mean you stop watching—it means an easier life while staying aware.

- Mark Your Calendar: Set up notices for yearly bills so you're ready for them.

Top tip: Use one card just for things you pay for often. If you need to stop or change something, you know just where to go.

Step 4: Pay Off Debt on Auto

Debt grows even as you sleep. Auto pay makes sure you're paying it down as you dream, too.

- Main-Target First: Pay tiny bits on all debts, then auto send extra money to the debt with the highest interest first.

- Small Wins: If staying on track is hard, start with your smallest debt. Quick wins help push you forward.

- Round-Up Apps: Some apps round your buys to the nearest dollar and move the extra cents towards your debt.

Example: An engineer I met auto-sends an extra $300 to his card debt each month. He says it's like "tossing water on a flame before it spreads."

Step 5: Keep Your Wealth Safe on Auto

Getting wealthy is just part of the job—keeping it is just as key.

- Auto Insurance Payments: Missed coverage can be huge trouble. Auto-pay your life, health, and property bills.

- Back-Ups Often: Set auto backups for key papers like wills and passwords.

- Fraud Alerts: Many banks can send you auto alerts for big buys, helping you catch fraud early.

Step 6: The Auto Magic

The beauty of setting things to auto is how it builds up. Here's how it spins:

1. Savings grow on their own.

1. Investments build your wealth on their own.

1. Bills get taken care of without you.

1. The time and brain power you save can go into making more or just living life.

Over time, this builds a cycle that feeds itself. Lisa—the teacher we talked about—now calls this her "quiet helper." Every day, her setup works harder than she does.

The Takeaway: Wealth Without Friction

MACHINES DON'T TAKE away smart thinking—they take away unevenness. By setting your money to run on its own, you cut out the need to make many small choices each day. Your cash shifts quietly, in a way you can count on, working hard without a sound.

True freedom isn't just about getting money—it's about making a strong plan where you don't have to think about money anymore. Then, you can think about life instead.

Chapter 14 — The Freedom Lifestyle Design

When Jordan turned thirty-five, he found out something worrying: he had cash, but no free time. His days were full of talks he didn't like, his email was a mess, and his weekends slipped away with tasks and tiredness. One night, as he looked at holiday snaps he never took, he said, "I'm full of stress, but empty of free time."

That night, he made a big change. Jordan stopped asking, "How can I earn more?" and started asking, "What life do I want, and how can money help me live it?"

This is what the Freedom Lifestyle is about—changing the game so money helps your life, not runs it.

The Core Idea: Money as a Tool, Not a Master

MANY FOLKS DON'T KNOW that their money choices shape their life. They get homes that hold them back, cars that need non-stop paying, or jobs that keep them stuck in one place. Real wealth is not just in money—it's in choices.

Freedom Lifestyle Design starts with one big, strong question:

If money were not a worry, what would you do with your time, and how would your days be?

Then, you plan your money to fit that dream.

Step 1: Set What Freedom Means to You

Let go of what folks think (big house, fancy car). Here's what it could look like for you:

- You Rule Your Time: How many hours in your day are yours?
- Choose Where to Live: Can you live where you love, not just work?
- Happy Work: Are you doing things that make you happy, not just for money?
- Money Stress: Can you handle big money trouble without losing peace?

What to do now: Map out your "Perfect Tuesday." What looks like a normal but great Tuesday for you? Write down your waking time, work details, and who you're with. Make this your guide.

Step 2: Make Money That Lets You Move

Cash is key to freedom, but not all cash works the same. Making money from a desk job isn't as good as earning from anywhere.

- Work from Home: Ask for remote work days. Even two days at home per week saves commute time and gives you freedom.
- Turn Skills into Products: Don't just work for cash, create things you can sell—courses, books, designs, or members-only stuff.
- Live Where It's Cheaper: Make money in strong currencies like USD or EUR and live somewhere cheap. You can live well on less.

Real story: A couple ran a small agency, but took it remote. They moved from New York City to Portugal, cut costs in half, and got a better life.

Step 3: Careful Spending for What Matters

Freedom isn't about giving things up; it's about spending smart.

- Check Added Costs: Drop what doesn't help you stay free. A car may lock you down; biking or car-sharing can free you up.
- Less Is More: Every canceled plan saves time and money.
- Buy Help, Not Things: Pay for chores to free up your time for better work or rest.

Think of it like trimming a tree. Every cut helps more important things grow.

Step 4: Plan How You Work

Freedom isn't quitting work; it's working as you choose.

- Work Hard, Then Rest: Put in solid work for 3 months, then take a break.
- Necessary Work Only: Find the most important 20% of your work and focus on that. Automate or drop the rest.
- Set Work Hours: Don't let work spread all day. Stop at set times to focus.

Try this: Work non-stop for 4 hours. No emails, just important stuff. It's surprising how freeing this is.

Step 5: Keep Your Freedom Safe

Freedom feels risky without backup. Set rules so you're not one emergency from trouble.

- Emergency Cash = Freedom Cash: Think of this like cash that lets you quit jobs you hate.

- Insurance = Freedom: Health and other insurance can keep one bad event from ruining everything.

- Quitting Fund: Even if you like your job, save up 6–12 months of costs. Nothing feels better than being able to just say no.

Step 6: Keep Changing Your Plan

What you think freedom is will change. What's exciting at twenty isn't the same at forty.

- Check your Perfect Tuesday yearly. Is it the same?

- Check your binds. Are you living your dream or someone else's?

- Keep updating your freedom plan, like software, always improving.

The Takeaway: Freedom Is Built, Not Found

JORDAN, THE BUSY GUY we talked about, now enjoys surfing in the morning before he starts his work from home. He makes a bit less money than when he was in the office, but he has more free time, less stress, and he controls his life.

Here's the key: freedom doesn't just show up at the end. It's something you make on purpose—by choosing how you make, use, and keep your stuff safe.

True wealth means being able to wake up every day and think: "Today, I live the way I want."

Chapter 15 — The Compounding Effect: Small Wins, Big Results

When Maya was 25, she began to save just $5 a day in an index fund. Her friends made fun of her—"That's just like buying coffee!"—but she kept at it. Jump to 20 years later: that small act grew to over $70,000, all due to compounding. Those friends who said they'd start later never got the same results.

What's the lesson? Being rich doesn't come from big jumps—it comes from tiny, steady steps that grow big over time.

This is the Compounding Effect—the unseen power that changes small choices into big results. It works with money, skills, ties with others, and even health. Once you use it on purpose, it turns into your best tool for building wealth.

The Core Idea: Why Compounding Works Like Magic

ADDING UP ISN'T JUST about more cash over time—it's about growth on top of more growth. Every small win sets up the next one. As time goes on, things start slow, then boom.

- In money talk: $100 put in each month with an 8% gain turns into $150,000 after 30 years. The same cash just kept in a jar? Only $36,000.

- With skills: If you learn one new way to write every week, you'll be great after some years of doing it.

- With habits: Reading 10 pages each day means you get through 12–15 books a year.

It's clear — adding up pays off for those who stick with it, not those who go all out at once.

STEP 1: BREAK YOUR Wins Into Small Pieces

The big trap is making goals too big to keep up with. Growth builds on doing a bit each day, not all at once.

- Don't go for a 5-mile run yet; start with 10 minutes.

- Don't aim to save $1000 each month; start with $50 or $100.

- Don't begin with a big business; try a simple $20 idea.

Small wins are easy. They're the tiny drops that make an ocean.

Do this: Set a "bare minimum habit." What is the smallest thing you can do every day to make headway? (for instance, write 100 words, do 5 push-ups, save $5).

Step 2: Make It Automatic to Save Willpower

Missing steps kill growth. That's why making things automatic helps.

- Money: Set up your paycheck to go into savings right when it hits. Think of saving like paying rent—it's a must.

- Learning: Set aside 15 minutes each day to learn a bit. Over time, that adds up to a lot.

- Networking: Set a weekly alert to connect with someone. Over time, these bonds grow strong.

For example, an entrepreneur put 10% of his pay into stocks that pay part of his money back. He didn't notice the money going out, but in 5 years, the extra money paid for his car. That's growth in action.

Step 3: Link Wins in Different Places

Growth speeds up when you mix your efforts.

- Money + Skills: Learn more to earn more. Reinvest that money for more growth.

- Health + Work: A daily workout lifts energy, which sharpens focus and speeds up success.

- Friends + Money: Building trust leads to chances you can't plan for.

Imagine habits as gears. When they work together, they move you forward much faster than alone.

Step 4: Hang in Through the Boring Part

The tough part is when you don't see quick results. That's when people give up.

- The first $1,000 may seem small.

- No one may read your first blog post.

- Early workouts might not show much.

But keep at it, things will take off.

Plan: Focus on ongoing actions, not just results. Track how many times you keep going, not just the final goal. The journey counts.

Step 5: Use Boosters

Growth quickens when you use boosters—choices that increase your small wins.

- Skill Booster: Learning to speak well betters talking, leading, and selling skills.
- Money Booster: Saving in tax-smart ways grows money quicker since you lose less to taxes.
- Relationship Booster: Helping others lifts your image, reach, and openings.

Ask: What small step today helps in many ways later?

Step 6: Guard the Growth

Care is key—it builds slowly but can fall apart fast with a poor choice.

- High-cost debts are like reverse growth.
- A rush bet can kill steady savings.
- Bad bonds can harm good networks.

Keep in mind: Avoid risks you can't fix. Growth comes from steady steps, not big bets.

Real-Life Example: The $10,000 Rule

THINK ABOUT BEN, WHO put $300 away each month, starting at age 20. By age 40, he had around $230,000. His pal Alex began at 30, putting in the same cash each month. By 40, Alex had only $52,000.

Why the big gap? Just 10 years of getting a head start. Ben put in only $36,000 more, but the growth over time made him nearly $180,000 richer. That's the true cost of putting things off.

The Takeaway: Win Small, Win Big

COMPOUNDING ISN'T ALL about the show. It's not quick or eye-catching. Yet, it's the top tool for making both cash and a good life, open to all.

Begin tiny. Keep at it. Guard your gains. Add boosters. And, big point, let it sit.

As time goes on, way down the road, some will see your life and say, "lucky." Yet, you'll get that it wasn't just a chance. It was the soft, hidden might of compounding—your tiny wins built up to big things.

Conclusion — Your Capital Flight Plan in Action

On a cold day in Chicago, James sat in his car by his work site, looking at the same dull walls he had seen for fifteen years. His job was ok, his pay was fine, but his life felt like it was on repeat: work, bills, taxes, over and over. One day, at lunch, a pal said she was going to stop working in her early forties—not by luck, but with a clear plan.

At first, James just laughed. But then, he couldn't stop thinking about it. That night, he opened his laptop, looked at the numbers, and saw that being free wasn't about making a ton of money; it was about making a plan that worked for him.

Five years on, James had cut his costs, set his savings to auto, made new ways to get cash, and had moved to Portugal for its cheaper living costs and better life. He wasn't "rich" in the old way, but he was free. And that's what this book aims to do: to help you make your version of James's story.

The Core Idea: Your Plan Is More Powerful Than Your Paycheck

IN THESE PARTS, WE'VE shown that you don't need huge luck, a big fortune, or a big tech public offer to get rich. Instead, we made a plan called the Capital Flight Plan: a clear way to stop running in place and start living as you want.

Let's make the key points clear:

1 Money Goes Where You Send It. Each dollar you make is a fighter. Use them smart—in investments, skills, and systems that help you.

2 Taxes Can Help, Not Just Take. Rich folks don't fear taxes—they get ready for them. And so can you.

3 Less Stuff Means More Wealth. Every buy you don't need holds you back. Skipping it isn't losing—it's gaining.

4 Think World-Wide to Open Paths. Chances are, out there, far from your home area. Living, working, or putting money in different places can speed up your progress.

5 Use Automation, Growth, and Small Gains as Helpers. Freedom comes with ongoing small steps, not just one big break.

The First Step Is Always Smaller Than You Think

YOU MAY FEEL IT'S TOO much now. Fifteen chapters of plans, ideas, and thoughts — where to start?

Start small.

- Open a new account and put in $50 every month by itself.
- Stop paying for one thing you don't use.
- Learn about one world chance (a visa, a bank, or a money move you didn't know about).
- Check what you own for the first time — the number isn't key, starting is.

Your plan isn't to do it all now. It's to build up little, sure wins until nothing can stop you.

Your Flight Plan Checklist

1. Find Your Freedom Number. What cash do you need each month to live as you wish? Note it. It's where you're headed.

1. Check Your Spending. Where does each buck go now? Knowing is how you stay in charge.

1. Use Tax Tips. Fill up retirement plans, use legal breaks, and look into credits just for you.

1. Set Up Auto Money Growth. Put money in savings and investments first without thinking. Make it easy.

1. Make Life Simple. Drop what doesn't help you. Each cut cost moves you nearer to freedom.

1. Spread Out Worldwide. Think about buying abroad, spending in other places, or even moving.

1. Make Your Trip Safe. Use insurance, save for emergencies, and mix it up.

1. Plan for Freedom, Not Just Old Age. Old age isn't just a number—it's a choice. Plan your life's path now.

1. Count Steps, Not Just Wins. Make the most of compound growth. Check every few months, not every day.

1. Keep Learning, Keep Changing. Markets switch, chances

come, and you will change. Fix the plan as you go.

Real-Life Examples: Proof It Works

- Angela, aged 34: Left her day job and set up a small shop on Etsy. With some smart tools and simple living, her $2,000 a month went a long way when she moved to Mexico City.

- Robert, aged 52: Used sharp tax moves and property buys to pay for his daily life. He didn't quit working early, but now he works as a consultant when he wants.

- Lena, aged 29: Worked on little wins each day—paid off her debts, put small cash in stocks, and read for 20 minutes a day. In five years, she knew a lot about money. She became the money expert in her house, and she's now using her money to buy her first house.

EACH TALE IS ITS OWN, yet the rule holds: steady steps + wise plans = freedom.

Your Future Self Is Already Waiting

THINK OF THIS: FIVE years ahead. You wake up with no alarm. Your day is full of things you want to do. You might be doing a job you love, just part-time. Or, you might be traveling. Or, just sitting with a cup of coffee on your porch, no worry about bills.

That dream isn't just a dream. It's a place you can reach. Your Capital Flight Plan is your guide.

But, like any plan, it starts when you begin the journey.

Final Call to Action

AS WE END THIS READ, think: you don't need a 'yes' from big money, your boss, or anyone else to start. You have the tools. You have the plan.

It's your turn now.

. Begin little.

. Keep at it.

. Believe in the power of growth.

Freedom doesn't come in one big jump. It comes in many small steps, each one moving you away from the start and toward the dream you made.

So strap in. It's time to steer your money toward freedom.

Your path is set. The question is: are you ready?

Bonus Section — The 90-Day Wealth Sprint Challenge

When Maya finally decided she was done with "someday thinking," she didn't start with a 10-year plan. She didn't overhaul her entire lifestyle overnight. Instead, she gave herself a 90-day window. Just three months to see what could change if she committed fully.

She tracked every expense, set up automatic investments, canceled a handful of subscriptions, and dedicated 30 minutes each day to building a side hustle she had been putting off.

By the end of those 90 days, she wasn't rich. But she was different. Her savings rate had doubled, she had $1,200 invested that wasn't there before, and her side hustle brought in its first $500. More importantly, she had proof: **momentum beats motivation.**

That's what this section is about. The **90-Day Wealth Sprint Challenge** is not about perfection—it's about acceleration. You won't retire in three months, but you'll build a foundation that makes early freedom inevitable.

Why 90 Days?

- It's long enough to see real change.
- It's short enough to keep sharp and not wear out.
- It makes you act now—no more "later," just a set end date.

SEE THIS AS A MONEY-making boot camp: quick, strong, and life-changing.

The Framework: Three 30-Day Blocks

We'll break the challenge into three parts, each building on the last.

Phase 1 (Days 1–30): Check and Attack

This month is for a clear start. You're not here to get rich fast—you're here to see things well.

Action Steps:

1. Watch Every Buck. Use a simple app (like Mint, YNAB, or even a sheet). Knowing gives you power.

1. Cut Clear Waste. Drop 2–3 costs you don't use. Streaming spots, gym tags you ignore, quick buys online.

1. Make Your Safety Net. Try to put away $500–$1,000 in a top savings bank spot. This helps if things go badly.

1. Set Your First Money Move. Even if it's $25 a week into an index fund, begin now.

Sprint Goal: Make 15–20% of your money each month free for saving or putting in.

Phase 2 (Days 31–60): Grow and Tune

With a clear view, speed it up.

Action Steps:

1. Talk Down a Big Bill. Call your net, phone, or cover folks. Even $20 a month less is $240 a year saved.

2. Grow Auto-Pays. Set auto sends to funds right after pay comes in. See it as fixed costs.

3. Start a Small Side Job. Choose a quick way to make cash:

○ Use your skills on Fiverr or Upwork.

○ Sell things you don't use on Facebook Marketplace.

○ Teach, help, or guide in what you know best.

4. Learn More. Spend 20 mins a day on reading, hearing, or studying how to build wealth.

Sprint Goal: Make at least $100–$500 more from new ways and fix in auto investing.

Phase 3 (Days 61–90): Broaden and Set

Now, shift from fast to long-term. You're making habits that will stick.

Action Steps:

1. Make a Plan for Your Side Job. If your small job made you $100, design a weekly way to grow it.

1. Look Worldwide. Study at least one outside chance—be it cost-saving living, a bank out there, or a job far but pays in bucks while you live cheap.

1. Create Your "Wealth Cycle." This means every saved or made buck goes into funds. For example: $200 saved + $200 made

= $400 a month into funds = $4,800 a year.

1. Check and Adjust. Look at your past 90 days. What did well? What was hard? Keep the good, drop the rest.

Sprint Goal: Have a set flow of cash building wealth, backed by a way to earn and spend smart.

Clever Strategies to Supercharge Your Sprint

- The 24-Hour Rule: Hold off for one day on any "must-buy" over $50. Most "needs" fade by the next day.

- The Swap Rule: When you get a new monthly pay plan, end an old one. This stops extra spending.

- Pay Trick: Set up a second bank spot. Move a set part (10-20%) of each pay into it. What you don't see gets saved without fuss.

- The Buddy System: Pair up your goals with a pal or your other half. Meet each week to talk. This helps both of you stay on track.

Real-Life Results You Can Expect

PEOPLE WHO HAVE TRIED this before saw things like:

- Daniel, 28: Cut $400 each month from what he spent, moved it to ETFs. In three months, he had $1,200 in and felt sure about his money like never before.

- Sofia, 41: Talked down her car insurance and cable bills, saving $1,000 a year. Used the extra money to pay off her credit card debt quickly.

- Marcus, 35: Made his weekend love of photos into a $300 a month extra job. That cash now goes into his Roth IRA.

The amounts differ, but the big change is the same: clear mind, in charge, and moving forward.

Your Turn: The Sprint Starts Now

THINK ABOUT WHERE YOU could be in 90 days if you begin now:

. You'll know exactly where each penny goes.

. You'll have money growing silently.

. You'll make a bit more cash on the side.

. You'll feel in charge—like you're flying, not just along for the ride.

You don't need a perfect plan. You need a sharp, short run.

The next three months will pass no matter what. The thing to ask is: will you still be at the same spot, or will you be looking back on 90 days of push that moved your path?

The path is open. The engines are set. Your 90-Day Wealth Sprint Challenge starts today.

www.ingramcontent.com/pod-product-compliance
Lightning Source LLC
LaVergne TN
LVHW022115200926
848481LV00003B/1175